EXO PLANETS

A GUIDE TO THE WORLDS OUTSIDE OUR SOLAR SYSTEM

Text copyright © 2023 by Wendy Bjazevich.

Illustration copyright © 2023 by David Miles.

Published by Bushel & Peck Books, a family-run publishing house in Fresno,
California, who believes in uplifting children with the highest standards of art, music,
literature, and ideas. For every book we sell, we donate one to a child in need—book for book.
To nominate a school or organization to receive free books, or to find inspiring books and gifts,
please visit www.bushelandpeckbooks.com.

ISBN: 9781638190981   LCCN: TK

First Edition

Printed in China

10 9 8 7 6 5 4 3 2

Collage illustrations, unless otherwise noted, created from textures and visuals sourced from Shutterstock.com.

Type set in Bebas, Josefin Sans, and Gill Sans Nova Inline.

EXO PLANETS

A GUIDE TO THE WORLDS OUTSIDE OUR SOLAR SYSTEM

WENDY BJAZEVICH • ART BY DAVID MILES

BUSHEL
& PECK
BOOKS

FRESNO, CALIFORNIA

CONTENTS

PART 1

AN INTRODUCTION TO EXOPLANETS

—

Did you know that there are billions of planets outside our own solar system? These planets are called extrasolar planets, or exoplanets for short. What are they like? How do we find them? Could they have life? Let's find out!

1

What is an exoplanet?

For years, scientists have been studying our solar system. They've taken pictures and gathered facts. From Mercury to Neptune, we have learned a lot about the planets in our system.

But did you know that there are planets, maybe even trillions of planets, outside our solar system? These planets are called exoplanets. Scientists describe an exoplanet as any planet that is beyond our solar system.

Most exoplanets orbit other stars, but some don't. Rogue planets are exoplanets that are untethered to any star, which means they are free-floating planets that drift.

The first exoplanets were discovered in the early 1990s. Since then, the number of confirmed exoplanets is in the thousands and rising.

STRANGE PLANETS

NASA tells us that there's a huge amount of variety among exoplanets. Some of these worlds sound very different from our Earth, like lava planets, water worlds, planets with multiple suns, and even worlds that are egg-shaped!

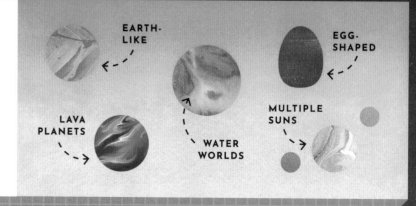

EARTH-LIKE

EGG-SHAPED

LAVA PLANETS

WATER WORLDS

MULTIPLE SUNS

1

A star is what planets orbit around. It is a source of heat and light. Our sun is a star.

2

A solar system is made up of a star and all of its orbiting planets, moons, asteroids, comet material, rocks, and dust. A solar system can have more than one star. Our solar system is made of our one star, the sun, and everything bound to it by gravity. Our solar system is the only system known to support life so far.

3

A galaxy is a collection of solar systems. Our galaxy is called the Milky Way Galaxy. Galaxies can come in many different sizes.

The universe is everything—all the galaxies put together. It contains billions of galaxies, including our Milky Way Galaxy. Scientists don't know the exact size of the universe, but they believe it is expanding.

4

HOW IS SPACE ORGANIZED?

An explanation of some of the terms scientists often use when studying exoplanets is helpful. From smallest to largest, these are: **1** star, **2** solar system, **3** galaxy, and **4** universe.

2 Why search for exoplanets?

LAUNCHED IN 2022, THE WEBB SPACE TELESCOPE IS EXPECTED TO FUNDAMENTALLY CHANGE OUR UNDERSTANDING OF EXOPLANETS. IT'S AN EXCITING TIME TO EXPLORE!

Beyond just curiosity, there are valuable reasons why scientists search for exoplanets. For one thing, experts can learn more about our solar system and Earth itself by comparing them to other planetary systems. Exoplanet observation can also help scientists discover how well they understand certain processes like planet formation and development.

However, planet discovery is perhaps most important because it opens up a massive area to look for habitable worlds in. Finding unmistakable signs of current life is the ultimate goal of NASA's exoplanet program. Scientists have probed our solar system for life, but so far, Earth is the only planet where it can be found.

Experts don't know how easily life begins, if it is rare or common, or how long it might last. But discovering exoplanets may help answer some of these questions.

It is possible that some of these exoplanets may have life or could provide a suitable place for life.

Today, even though scientists still have many more questions than answers, they are closer to answering the question of whether we are alone in the universe.

TYPES OF EXOPLANETS

Exoplanets come in a wide variety of sizes. Both mass and size play an essential role in determining exoplanet type. Varieties within the mass/size classifications also exist.

So far, scientists have categorized exoplanets into four main types: **1** Gas Giant (very large, composed mainly of gas) **2** Neptune-like/Neptunian (gaseous, around the size of Neptune) **3** Super-Earth (potentially rocky, larger than Earth) and **4** Terrestrial (rocky, outside our solar system, Earth-sized or smaller).

1

GAS GIANT

3

NEPTUNIAN

2

SUPER-EARTH

4

TERRESTRIAL

3 How we find new planets

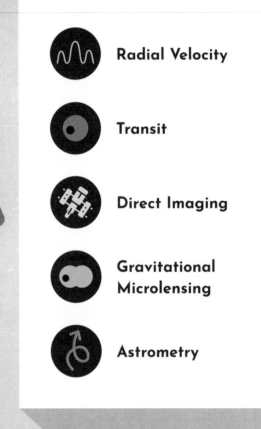

Scientists think that almost every star in our galaxy has at least one planet orbiting it. Over the last few decades, scientists have discovered and named thousands of planets outside our solar system.

These exoplanets come in a wide variety of sizes and orbits, but one thing they all have in common is that they are light-years away from Earth. In fact, even with powerful telescopes, few exoplanets have had their pictures taken. So how do scientists know all those planets are out there?

Because exoplanets are so distant, dim, and difficult to discover, exoplanet-hunting scientists have had to be creative. Nearly all the exoplanets discovered so far have been found indirectly.

METHODS OF DISCOVERY

According to NASA, there are five main methods that scientists use to discover exoplanets:

- **Radial Velocity**
- **Transit**
- **Direct Imaging**
- **Gravitational Microlensing**
- **Astrometry**

I LIGHT-YEAR

JAN FEB MAR APR MAY JUN JUL AUG SEP OCT NOV DEC

HOW FAR IS A LIGHT-YEAR?

A light-year is the distance that light can travel in the space of one year (and light travels *really* fast!). Put another way, it's about 6,000,000,000,000 miles, or around 240 million times around the Earth. That's far!

DISCOVERY METHOD 1:
RADIAL VELOCITY

In 1995, scientists discovered the first exoplanet orbiting a star like our sun. They named it 51 Pegasi b (see page 27).

(see page 27).

51 Pegasi b was discovered using what is now called the radial velocity method. When a large planet orbits near a star, the planet exerts its gravity on the star and makes it shift, or wobble, ever so slightly. NASA has described it as a gravitational "tug-of-war."

When the star moves, the appearance of the light energy emmitted by the star changes. Energy moves like waves, and those waves can be squeezed or stretched, depending on the movement of the object making them (this is called the Doppler effect). Changes in wavelength change how we perceive the energy we're seeing. When visible light waves scrunch together, they look more blue. When visible light waves stretch out, they look more red.

When a star wobbles, the light waves scrunch together and then stretch out, changing the color of the light back and forth between blue and red. This tells scientists that something large is moving around the star. What could it be? You guessed it, a planet!

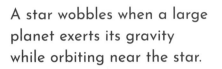

A star wobbles when a large planet exerts its gravity while orbiting near the star.

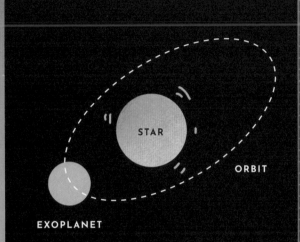

STAR

ORBIT

EXOPLANET

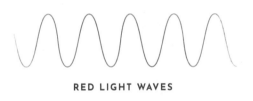

RED LIGHT WAVES

BLUE LIGHT WAVES

Scientists look for a star that changes color, indicating that something large nearby is creating those fluctuations.

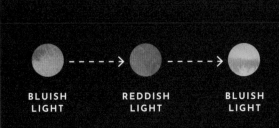

BLUISH LIGHT → REDDISH LIGHT → BLUISH LIGHT

STAR

TRANSITING PLANET

Light curves measure the brightness of a star over time. A dip in brightness is a good clue that something—maybe a planet!—moved in front.

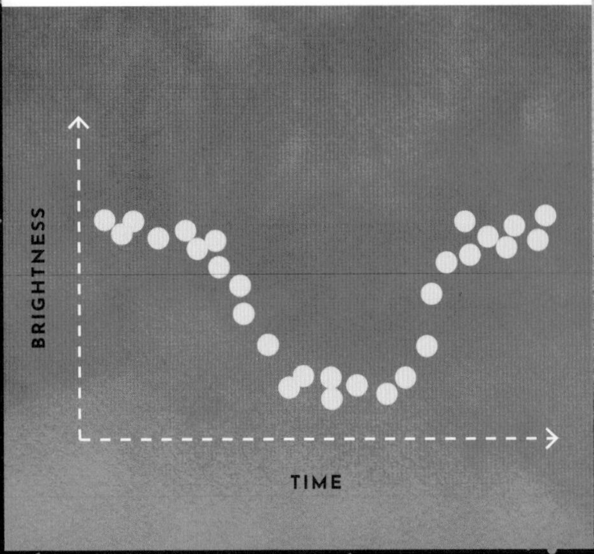

DISCOVERY METHOD 2:
TRANSIT

The transit method has been very successful in finding new exoplanets. A transit occurs when a planet passes between a star and its observer. As a planet transits (or moves) in front of a star, it blocks a little bit of the star's light and dims the star's brightness by an amount that can be measured. In this way, a transit reveals exoplanets not because the planet can actually be seen, but because the planet dims the light of the star it is passing in front of.

Experts make a graph called a light curve, which can show any variation of light observed from a star over a period of time. A repeating dip in the star's brightness might indicate an exoplanet moving in a regular orbit around that star.

BRIGHTNESS

TIME

READING STARLIGHT

The transit method can also help to determine other characteristics of an exoplanet, such as the size of the planet and the planet's distance from the sun. Studying the starlight that passes through a transiting planet's atmosphere can even help scientists determine what the atmosphere is made of.

DISCOVERY METHOD 3:
DIRECT IMAGING

Exoplanets are very far away. They are often much dimmer than the stars they orbit, so they can be lost in the glare of their host star's massive amounts of radiation. Quite often, exoplanets are so distant and dim that they are practically invisible. That's the reason most of the exoplanets so far have been discovered using methods that rely on the planets' effect on the stars they orbit.

However, new technology is helping to solve many of the problems direct imaging has faced. Using two new techniques—coronography and starshade—scientists can block out some of the starlight and catch glimpses of the hidden planets.

CORONOGRAPHY

Coronography uses a device inside a telescope to block the overwhelming light of a star (the green X below) so the exoplanets in orbit around it (the colored shapes) can be revealed. Coronagraphs are being used to directly image exoplanets from ground-based observatories.

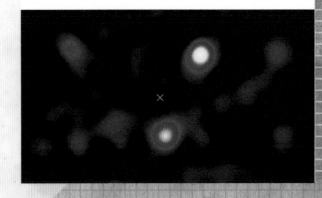

SOURCE: NASA/JPL-CALTECH/PALOMAR OBSERVATORY

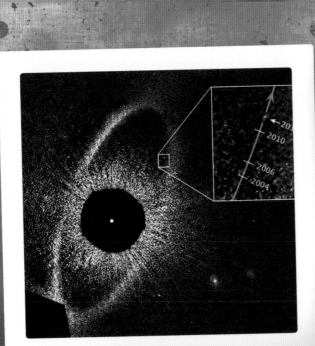

FOMALHAUT SYSTEM

By blocking out the star's light, the Hubble Space Telescope was able to capture the orbital movement of the exoplanet Fomalhaut b.

SOURCE: NASA, ESA, AND P. KALAS

STARSHADE

A starshade is a sunflower-shaped spacecraft about the size of a baseball diamond. Still in the design phase, it's thought that a starshade could be used to block starlight before it enters a space-based telescope. This device can be positioned in just the right place to block a star's light from where astronomers are observing. It will be exciting to see this development come to life!

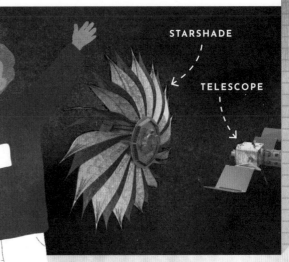

STARSHADE

TELESCOPE

SOURCE: NASA/JPL-CALTECH

As the rogue planet moves near the star, the light from the star warps, creating a double image.

As the double image overlaps, the star's brightness appears to increase.

The brightness diminishes as the planet passes and the double image separates.

Unlike the transit method, when using gravitational microlensing, scientists look for an *increase* in a star's brightness.

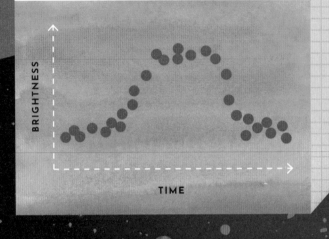

BRIGHTNESS

TIME

DISCOVERY METHOD 4:

GRAVITATIONAL MICROLENSING

Gravitational microlensing uses the effect of gravity on light. This effect was described first by Albert Einstein and involves gravity's ability to warp and bend starlight.

While the gravitational microlensing method can sometimes be used to discover exoplanets that orbit around a host star, this method is particularly useful for discovering rogue planets (those that *don't* orbit a star).

Rogue planets are usually much harder to find. But if a rogue exoplanet aligns closely with a star and the star is at a farther distance than the exoplanet, from our viewpoint, the star's light will bend around the planet. When this happens, the rogue planet acts like a natural magnifying glass and the background star's light is amplified.

Astronomers can see and measure the effect of this amplification as a spike in the star's brightness. When spikes are detected, it's a good indication that there are rogue planets on the scene.

The Nancy Grace Roman Space Telescope, expected to launch in 2027, will likely be a game-changer for rogue planet searches because it is designed to conduct large microlensing surveys.

NANCY GRACE ROMAN SPACE TELESCOPE

ROGUE PLANET

DOUBLE IMAGE OVERLAPPING

ASTROMETRY

Astrometry, like radial velocity, looks for a wobbling star. It doesn't, however, look for the wobble using Doppler shift (those color changes due to fluctuations in wavelength). Rather, astrometry detects the motion of a star by making very precise measurements of the star's position in the sky. If a star has a planet orbiting it, the star's movement will be slightly different than if the star has no planet in orbit.

Astrometry is a very difficult technique to use because of the extreme accuracy that is needed to detect true changes in a star's movement. Sometimes, though, it is used as a follow-up technique after a planet has been detected by another method.

Unfortunately, because our atmosphere bends and distorts light, the astrometry method is very hard to use from the Earth's surface.

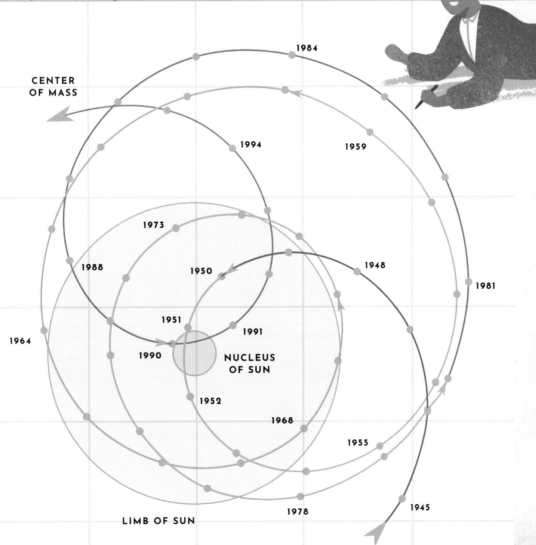

OUR STAR MOVES, TOO!

The chart on the left shows the movement of our sun between the years 1945 to 1995. Follow the trail starting at 1945 in the bottom right. The large yellow circle is the actual size of the sun. You can see how much it really moved around!

SOURCE: SOLAR SYSTEM BARYCENTRE ORBIT AROUND SUN BY CARL SMITH VIA WIKIMEDIA COMMONS

4 Could exoplanets have life?

Finding unmistakable signs of current life on a planet beyond Earth is the ultimate goal of NASA's exoplanet program. There are many questions. To begin with, where will experts look for life, how will they look, and is there a chance scientists will find it? Scientists are starting to narrow in on some of the answers using three powerful models.

THREE MODELS FOR FINDING LIFE

The Habitable Zone: The habitable zone is an area, or range from a star, where liquid water could exist on the surface of an orbiting planet. Searching for life where this water might be is an excellent place to start because experts believe such water could be key to life.

Spectroscopy: Light could also be central to how scientists look for life. Through spectroscopy, an exoplanet's atmosphere could tell experts a lot about the gases and chemicals in its sky.

Probability: With the discovery of each additional exoplanet, the math of probability offers a useful way to look at the likelihood of finding life.

THE HABITABLE ZONE

The idea of a "habitable zone" is one of the best tools scientists have today in their search for habitable exoplanets. It's a way for researchers to zero in on planets where life has the best chance of surviving. In a sense, it narrows the likely possibilities.

The habitable zone is the range from a star where liquid water could exist on an orbiting planet's surface. It's been called the Goldilocks Zone because the temperature in this zone might be just right for life—not too hot and not too cold.

TOO HOT

THE HABITABLE ZONE

TOO COLD

LIQUID WATER

32°F / 0°C
WATER FREEZES

212°F / 100°C
WATER BOILS AND
EVAPORATES

NOT JUST WATER

In addition to water, other conditions are necessary if any planet is going to be considered habitable. To start with, there must be a stable star and a planet of suitable size with a suitable atmosphere.

HOW MANY PLANETS ARE IN A HABITABLE ZONE?

Among the thousands of exoplanets discovered so far, dozens of them are considered to dwell in the habitable zone around their stars. Scientists believe there could be as many as 300 million planets in a habitable zone in our galaxy.

||||| SPECTROSCOPY

Even though exoplanets are very distant, we have discovered ways that we can learn about them. One of those ways is called spectroscopy. Put very simply, spectroscopy is reading light signatures for information.

Light is electromagnetic (EM) radiation. Like ripples through water, light moves like a wave through space. A wave's length determines its color, and scientists can tell a lot about an object by observing what color light the object reflects. Color can provide information about what a surface is, what something is made of, and even its temperature.

Spectroscopy is especially useful when trying to figure out what an exoplanet's atmosphere is made of. As a star's light passes through the atmosphere of a planet, the atoms and molecules of different materials absorb light at different wavelengths. When scientists analyze this light using spectroscopy, the effects look like a barcode. The slices missing from the light spectrum indicate which gases (like oxygen, hydrogen, or nitrogen) or chemicals are present in the atmosphere—the materials that would have absorbed parts of the light.

LIGHT'S FULL COLOR SPECTRUM LOOKS LIKE THIS WHEN IT GOES THROUGH A PRISM.

BUT WHEN LIGHT PASSES THROUGH A PLANET'S ATMOSPHERE, SOME OF THE PLANET'S ELEMENTS ABSORB PARTS OF THE LIGHT, LEAVING GAPS IN THE COLOR SPECTRUM.

SOURCE: NOAO, AURA/NSF, NASA, JPL-CALTECH, K. GORDON (UNIVERSITY OF ARIZONA)

SEEING INFRARED

Unfortunately, our unaided eyes can see only part of the electromagnetic spectrum. Luckily, special telescopes can detect the infrared part of the EM spectrum. Compare the visible-light image of the Andromeda galaxy on the left with its infrared image on the right. Quite a difference! In this way, infrared can uncover some of an exoplanet's invisible secrets.

PROBABILITY

Probability is a practical branch of mathematics that can be very useful in determining whether planets can support life.

Probability can be thought of as how likely something is to happen. This likelihood can actually be calculated.

A very simple example can be shown using a die. When a single die is thrown, there are six possible outcomes: 1, 2, 3, 4, 5, 6. The probability of any one of them happening is one out of six (1/6). The law of large numbers tells us that the more times we roll the die, the closer we will get to the outcome that we expected, one out of six (1/6).

With this understanding in place and the ever-increasing number of exoplanets being discovered (which means more planets to try), it seems more and more likely that there is at least one other planet that has the right conditions for life. Yet so far, the planet still eludes scientists.

IF YOU ROLL A DIE ONCE, THE CHANCE OF IT BEING A 6 IS 1/6.

IF YOU ROLL THE DIE MANY TIMES, YOU HAVE A MUCH HIGHER CHANCE OF GETTING A 6.

SCIENTISTS HAVE CONFIRMED OVER 5,000 EXOPLANETS, BUT THERE ARE BILLIONS IN JUST OUR GALAXY. THAT'S A LOT OF DIE ROLLS!

PART 2
MEET THE EXOPLANETS

—

So far, scientists have categorized exoplanets into four main groups: gas giant, Neptunian, super-Earth, and terrestrial. Learn how each of these planet types varies in its exterior and interior appearance, and meet some of the most famous ones in our galaxy!

5 Gas giants

A gas giant is a large planet made mostly of gas. Gas giants, like Jupiter and Saturn in our solar system, are made of mainly helium and/or hydrogen. Gas giant exoplanets can be similar in size or even much larger than the largest planet in our solar system, which is Jupiter.

Gas giants don't have a hard, well-defined surface like rocky planets do. Instead, they have swirling gases of mainly helium and/or hydrogen above a solid core. This solid core may be metallic or rocky. These planets can also be much closer to their stars than any of the planets found in our solar system.

BECAUSE OF THEIR MASSIVE SIZE, GAS GIANTS OFTEN HAVE ORBITING MOONS.

HOT JUPITERS

Gas giants close to their stars are often called "hot Jupiters." Hot Jupiters orbit so close to their stars that their temperatures can reach thousands of degrees (Fahrenheit or Celsius!). Described as scorching planets, one hot Jupiter, KELT-9 b, is so hot that molecules in its atmosphere are even torn apart.

Hot Jupiters were one of the first exoplanet types discovered. These gas giants make such tight orbits and are so large that they cause a more noticeable "wobble" in their stars. This wobble made hot Jupiters easier to find in the early days of planet-hunting using the radial velocity method (see page 13).

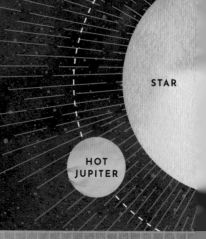

STAR

HOT JUPITER

LAYERS OF SWIRLING GASES (MOSTLY HELIUM AND/ OR HYDROGEN)

OLD PLANETS

Scientists believe that gas giants are among the first planets to form in a new solar system, perhaps within the first 10 million years of a sun's life.

MEET SOME GAS GIANTS

A

Earth

This was the first exoplanet to have its clouds mapped.

KEPLER-7 B

MASS: 0.441 Jupiters
ORBITAL RADIUS: 0.06067 AU
ECCENTRICITY: 0.0
DISCOVERY DATE: 2009
PLANET RADIUS: 1.622 x Jupiter
ORBITAL PERIOD: 4.9 days
DETECTION METHOD: Transit

B

Earth

WASP-12 b is so close to its star, it will be evaporated within 10 mil years.

WASP-12 B

MASS: 1.465 Jupiters
ORBITAL RADIUS: 0.0232 AU
ECCENTRICITY: 0.04
DISCOVERY DATE: 2008
PLANET RADIUS: 1.937 x Jupiter
ORBITAL PERIOD: 1.1 days
DETECTION METHOD: Trans

F

Earth

It takes over 600 years for this planet to orbit its star just one time!

HIP 65426 B

MASS: 9 Jupiters
ORBITAL RADIUS: 92.0 AU
ECCENTRICITY: 0.0
DISCOVERY DATE: 2017
PLANET RADIUS: 1.5 x Jupiter
ORBITAL PERIOD: 630.7 years
DETECTION METHOD: Direct Imaging

G

Earth

TOI-3757 b has the same density as a marshmallow.

TOI-3757 B

MASS: 0.26838 Jupiters
ORBITAL RADIUS: 0.03845 AU
ECCENTRICITY: 0.14
DISCOVERY DATE: 2022
PLANET RADIUS: 1.071 x Jupiter
ORBITAL PERIOD: 3.4 days
DETECTION METHOD: Transit

H

Earth

A year on this planet is close a year on Ear

11 COMAE BERENICES B

MASS: 19.4 Jupiters
ORBITAL RADIUS: 1.29 AU
ECCENTRICITY: 0.23
DISCOVERY DATE: 2007
PLANET RADIUS: 1.08 x Jupi
ORBITAL PERIOD: 326 days
DETECTION METHOD: Radial Velocity

L

Earth

HIP 67522 B

MASS: 0.228 Jupiters
ORBITAL RADIUS: Unknown
ECCENTRICITY: 0.06
DISCOVERY DATE: 2020
PLANET RADIUS: 0.898 x Jupiter
ORBITAL PERIOD: 7 days
DETECTION METHOD: Transit

M

Earth

AB AURIGAE B

MASS: 9 Jupiters
ORBITAL RADIUS: 93.9 AU
ECCENTRICITY: 0.4
DISCOVERY DATE: 2022
PLANET RADIUS: 1.12 x Jupiter
ORBITAL PERIOD: 587.7 years
DETECTION METHOD: Direct Imaging

N

Earth

YSES 2 b's hos star is a young sun.

YSES 2 B

MASS: 6.3 Jupiters
ORBITAL RADIUS: 115.0 AU
ECCENTRICITY: 0.0
DISCOVERY DATE: 2021
PLANET RADIUS: 1.14 x Jupit
ORBITAL PERIOD: 1,176.5 ye
DETECTION METHOD: Direct Imaging

R

Earth

KELT-9 b is so hot on the dayside, its molecules are literally pulled apart by the intensity. (They reform on the nightside.)

KELT-9 B

MASS: 2.88 Jupiters
ORBITAL RADIUS: 0.03462 AU
ECCENTRICITY: 0.0
DISCOVERY DATE: 2017
PLANET RADIUS: 1.891 x Jupiter
ORBITAL PERIOD: 1.5 days
DETECTION METHOD: Transit

S

Earth

Kepler-16 b has twin suns, just like Tatooine from *Star Wars*!

KEPLER-16 B

MASS: 0.333 Jupiters
ORBITAL RADIUS: 0.7048 AU
ECCENTRICITY: 0.01
DISCOVERY DATE: 2011
PLANET RADIUS: 0.754 x Jupiter
ORBITAL PERIOD: 228.8 days
DETECTION METHOD: Transit

T

Earth

Kepler-7 b cou float (if you had a tub big enough, that is!). Its density about the sam as Styrofoam.

KEPLER-7 B

MASS: 0.441 Jupiters
ORBITAL RADIUS: 0.06067 AU
ECCENTRICITY: 0.0
DISCOVERY DATE: 2009
PLANET RADIUS: 1.622 x Jupiter
ORBITAL PERIOD: 4.9 days
DETECTION METHOD: Transit

The Webb telescope discovered signs of water in WASP-96 b's atmosphere in 2022.

WASP-96 B

- Earth

MASS: 0.48 Jupiters
ORBITAL RADIUS: 0.0453 AU
ECCENTRICITY: 0.0
DISCOVERY DATE: 2014

PLANET RADIUS: 1.2 x Jupiter
ORBITAL PERIOD: 3.4 days
DETECTION METHOD: Transit

D

The Webb telescope found the first clear sign of carbon dioxide in an exoplanet in WASP-39 b's atmosphere.

WASP-39 B

- Earth

MASS: 0.28 Jupiters
ORBITAL RADIUS: 0.0486 AU
ECCENTRICITY: 0.0
DISCOVERY DATE: 2011

PLANET RADIUS: 1.27 x Jupiter
ORBITAL PERIOD: 4.1 days
DETECTION METHOD: Transit

E

Also called "Mulchatna" after a salmon-rich river in Alaska.

HD 17156 B

- Earth

MASS: 3.51 Jupiters
ORBITAL RADIUS: 0.16278 AU
ECCENTRICITY: 0.68
DISCOVERY DATE: 2007

PLANET RADIUS: 1.1 x Jupiter
ORBITAL PERIOD: 21.2 days
DETECTION METHOD: Radial Velocity

TOI-2109 B

- Earth

MASS: 5.02 Jupiters
ORBITAL RADIUS: 0.01791 AU
ECCENTRICITY: 0.0
DISCOVERY DATE: 2021

PLANET RADIUS: 1.347 x Jupiter
ORBITAL PERIOD: 0.7 days
DETECTION METHOD: Transit

J

TOI-3362 B

- Earth

MASS: 5.029 Jupiters
ORBITAL RADIUS: 0.153 AU
ECCENTRICITY: 0.82
DISCOVERY DATE: 2021

PLANET RADIUS: 1.142 x Jupiter
ORBITAL PERIOD: 18.1 days
DETECTION METHOD: Transit

K

This was the first planet discovered around a sun-like star!

51 PEGASI B

- Earth

MASS: 0.46 Jupiters
ORBITAL RADIUS: 0.0527 AU
ECCENTRICITY: 0.01
DISCOVERY DATE: 1995

PLANET RADIUS: 1.27 x Jupiter
ORBITAL PERIOD: 4.2 days
DETECTION METHOD: Radial Velocity

This planet is so large, scientists believe it might even be a cluster of planets or a brown dwarf.

D 100546 B

- Earth

MASS: 752 Jupiters
ORBITAL RADIUS: 53.0 AU
ECCENTRICITY: 0.0
DISCOVERY DATE: 2014

PLANET RADIUS: 6.9 x Jupiter
ORBITAL PERIOD: 249.2 years
DETECTION METHOD: Direct Imaging

P

GJ 504 b is a deep pink color and likely still glowing from its birth as a planet.

GJ 504 B

- Earth

MASS: 4 Jupiters
ORBITAL RADIUS: 43.5 AU
ECCENTRICITY: 0.0
DISCOVERY DATE: 2013

PLANET RADIUS: 1.16 x Jupiter
ORBITAL PERIOD: 259.9 years
DETECTION METHOD: Direct Imaging

Q

Winds on this hazardous planet carry tiny, razor-sharp shards of glass.

HD 189733 B

- Earth

MASS: 1.13 Jupiters
ORBITAL RADIUS: 0.03126 AU
ECCENTRICITY: 0.0
DISCOVERY DATE: 2005

PLANET RADIUS: 1.13 x Jupiter
ORBITAL PERIOD: 2.2 days
DETECTION METHOD: Radial Velocity

TIC 172900988 b has two stars in its system, and maybe even three!

IC 172900988 B

- Earth

MASS: 2.96386 Jupiters
ORBITAL RADIUS: 0.90281 AU
ECCENTRICITY: 0.03
DISCOVERY DATE: 2021

PLANET RADIUS: 1.004 x Jupiter
ORBITAL PERIOD: 200.5 days
DETECTION METHOD: Transit

V

This planet's surface temperature is almost 2,800°F—three times hotter than Venus.

TOI-849 B

- Earth

MASS: 39.09 Earths
ORBITAL RADIUS: 0.01598 AU
ECCENTRICITY: 0.0
DISCOVERY DATE: 2020

PLANET RADIUS: 0.307 x Jupiter
ORBITAL PERIOD: 0.8 days
DETECTION METHOD: Transit

W

HAT-P-67 B

- Earth

MASS: 0.34 Jupiters
ORBITAL RADIUS: Unknown
ECCENTRICITY: 0.0
DISCOVERY DATE: 2017

PLANET RADIUS: 2.085 x Jupiter
ORBITAL PERIOD: 4.8 days
DETECTION METHOD: Transit

TYPE 2:

Neptunian

HOT
NEPTUNE

Neptunian exoplanets are similar in size to the planets Neptune or Uranus in our solar system. Hydrogen and helium dominate these exoplanets' outer atmospheres. Neptunian exoplanets likely have a mixture of interior compositions with rocky and heavier metal cores.
Neptunian exoplanets vary widely in size and usual distance from their stars. Scientists have discovered exoplanets smaller than Neptune and bigger than Earth; these planets are called mini-Neptunes. Most Neptune-sized exoplanets orbit farther away from their stars. But so-called hot Neptunes, exoplanets in a tight, fast orbit around their stars, have also been found. These exoplanets have extremely hot atmospheres, and only a small number have been discovered so far.

MINI-
NEPTUNE

NEPTUNIAN DESERTS

Neptunian Desert is the name given to the area close to stars where no large Neptune-sized planets are expected to survive long. Intense radiation is found in the Neptunian Desert, and this radiation can evaporate gaseous atmospheres until there is nothing left but rock. This suggests that hot Neptunes may be a class of planets in transition.

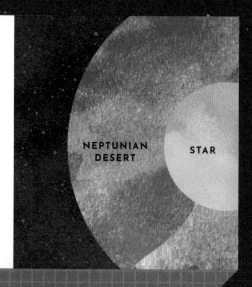

NEPTUNIAN
DESERT   STAR

TOUGH STUDIES

Thick clouds often block any light from coming through Neptunian exoplanets. This makes it more difficult to learn about their atmospheres using spectrometry. The new Webb Space Telescope, however, should be able to take a much better look at exoplanet atmospheres even through clouds.

CORE (PROBABLY MADE FROM ROCK AND HEAVY METALS)

LAYERS OF GAS, USUALLY HYDROGEN OR HELIUM

VISIBLE CLOUDS

TYPE 3:

Super-Earth

A super-Earth is a type of exoplanet unlike any in our solar system. These exoplanets are more massive than our Earth but lighter than Neptune and Uranus. Super-Earths may or may not have atmospheres and they can be made of rock, gas, or a combination of both.

The name super-Earth doesn't mean it's like Earth but better. The name simply refers to the exoplanets' size, which is larger than Earth and smaller than Neptune.

Though there aren't any in our own solar system, super-Earths are some of the most common planets discovered so far in our galaxy.

HOW BIG IS SUPER?

Super-Earth exoplanets can be up to 10 times the mass of Earth. Exoplanets toward the top of the size limit for a super-Earth can also be called mini- or sub-Neptunes.

EARTH

SUPER-EARTH
(UP TO 10X
IN SIZE)

VAPORIZED

Planet K2-131 b is a super-Earth that orbits a sun-like yellow star. This exoplanet isn't just a super-Earth—it's also superhot. Temperatures on this planet are hot enough to vaporize metal.

CORE

SUPER-EARTHS VARY IN COMPOSITION AND COULD BE ROCKY, GASEOUS, OR BOTH.

WEIRD WORLDS

There is a lot we don't know about super-Earths, but scientists believe some could be covered completely with water, others with snow and ice, and still others with molten metal!

WATER

SNOW AND ICE

MOLTEN METAL

MEET SOME NEPTUNIAN EXOPLANETS

A

Earth

HAT-P-26 b was first discovered with powerful telescopes in Arizona and Hawaii.

HAT-P-26 B

MASS: 22.2481 Earths
ORBITAL RADIUS: 0.0479 AU
ECCENTRICITY: 0.12
DISCOVERY DATE: 2010

PLANET RADIUS: 0.63 x Jupiter
ORBITAL PERIOD: 4.2 days
DETECTION METHOD: Transit

B

Earth

HAT-P-11 b's magnetosphe was discovere in 2021, the first for any exoplanet.

HAT-P-11 B

MASS: 26.69772 Earths
ORBITAL RADIUS: 0.05254 AU
ECCENTRICITY: 0.22
DISCOVERY DATE: 2008

PLANET RADIUS: 0.389 x Jupiter
ORBITAL PERIOD: 4.9 days
DETECTION METHOD: Transit

F

Earth

BD-06 1339 B

MASS: 8.5 Earths
ORBITAL RADIUS: 0.0428 AU
ECCENTRICITY: 0.0
DISCOVERY DATE: 2013

PLANET RADIUS: 0.254 x Jupiter
ORBITAL PERIOD: 3.9 days
DETECTION METHOD: Radial Velocity

G

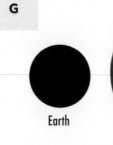

Earth

EPIC 212297394 C

MASS: 5.77 Earths
ORBITAL RADIUS: Unknown
ECCENTRICITY: 0.0
DISCOVERY DATE: 2016

PLANET RADIUS: 0.203 x Jupiter
ORBITAL PERIOD: 5.2 days
DETECTION METHOD: Transit

H

Earth

GJ 1214 B

MASS: 8.17 Earths
ORBITAL RADIUS: 0.0149 AU
ECCENTRICITY: < 0.063
DISCOVERY DATE: 2009

PLANET RADIUS: 0.245 x Jupiter
ORBITAL PERIOD: 1.6 days
DETECTION METHOD: Transit

MEET SOME SUPER-EARTHS

L

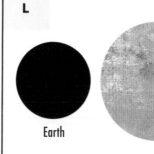

Earth

The temperature on this planet is around 530˚F.

GJ 15 A B

MASS: 3.03 Earths
ORBITAL RADIUS: 0.072 AU
ECCENTRICITY: 0.09
DISCOVERY DATE: 2014

PLANET RADIUS: 1.55 x Earth
ORBITAL PERIOD: 11.4 days
DETECTION METHOD: Radial Velocity

M

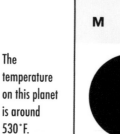

Earth

Though it once lost its atmosphere, G 1132 b is gain a new one fro gases being released by volcanic activit

GJ 1132 B

MASS: 1.66 Earths
ORBITAL RADIUS: 0.0153 AU
ECCENTRICITY: 0.22
DISCOVERY DATE: 2015

PLANET RADIUS: 1.13 x Earth
ORBITAL PERIOD: 1.6 days
DETECTION METHOD: Transit

Q

Earth

LHS 1140 B

MASS: 6.38 Earths
ORBITAL RADIUS: 0.0957 AU
ECCENTRICITY: < 0.096
DISCOVERY DATE: 2017

PLANET RADIUS: 1.635 x Earth
ORBITAL PERIOD: 24.7 days
DETECTION METHOD: Transit

R

Earth

KEPLER-334 D

MASS: 2.57 Earths
ORBITAL RADIUS: 0.168 AU
ECCENTRICITY: 0.0
DISCOVERY DATE: 2014

PLANET RADIUS: 1.41 x Earth
ORBITAL PERIOD: 25.1 days
DETECTION METHOD: Transit

S

Earth

KEPLER-7 B

MASS: 3.89 Earths
ORBITAL RADIUS: 0.414 AU
ECCENTRICITY: 0.0
DISCOVERY DATE: 2014

PLANET RADIUS: 1.8 x Earth
ORBITAL PERIOD: 91.4 days
DETECTION METHOD: Transit

Scientists think
the planet
may be made
of pressure-
hardened "ice."

436 B

MASS: 22.1 Earths
ORBITAL RADIUS: 0.0291 AU
ECCENTRICITY: 0.14
DISCOVERY DATE: 2004

PLANET RADIUS: 0.372 x Jupiter
ORBITAL PERIOD: 2.6 days
DETECTION METHOD: Radial Velocity

D

Earth

KEPLER-1625 B

MASS: 30.6 Earths
ORBITAL RADIUS: 0.8748 AU
ECCENTRICITY: 0.0
DISCOVERY DATE: 2016

PLANET RADIUS: 0.541 x Jupiter
ORBITAL PERIOD: 287.4 days
DETECTION METHOD: Transit

E

Earth

Sometimes called
"Hoth" by scientists,
this planet's surface
can reach −370°F!

OGLE-2005-BLG-390L B

MASS: 5.5 Earths
ORBITAL RADIUS: 2.6 AU
ECCENTRICITY: 0.0
DISCOVERY DATE: 2005

PLANET RADIUS: 2.21 x Earth
ORBITAL PERIOD: 9 years
DETECTION METHOD: Gravitational Microlensing

Earth

164922 E

MASS: 10.52012 Earths
ORBITAL RADIUS: 0.2292 AU
ECCENTRICITY: 0.09
DISCOVERY DATE: 2021

PLANET RADIUS: 0.288 x Jupiter
ORBITAL PERIOD: 41.8 days
DETECTION METHOD: Radial Velocity

J

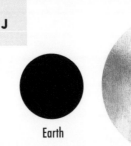

Earth

KEPLER-122 D

MASS: 5.48 Earths
ORBITAL RADIUS: 0.155 AU
ECCENTRICITY: 0.0
DISCOVERY DATE: 2014

PLANET RADIUS: 2.2 x Earth
ORBITAL PERIOD: 21.6 days
DETECTION METHOD: Transit

K

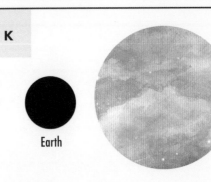

Earth

TOI-125 B

MASS: 9.5 Earths
ORBITAL RADIUS: 0.05186 AU
ECCENTRICITY: 0.19
DISCOVERY DATE: 2019

PLANET RADIUS: 0.243 x Jupiter
ORBITAL PERIOD: 4.7 days
DETECTION METHOD: Transit

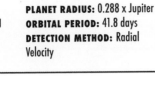

Earth

Kepler-452 b is a
most intriguing
planet. Its
size, shape,
star, orbit, and
position in its
solar system are
similar to those
of Earth!

KEPLER-452 B

MASS: 3.29 Earths
ORBITAL RADIUS: 1.046 AU
ECCENTRICITY: 0.0
DISCOVERY DATE: 2015

PLANET RADIUS: 1.63 x Earth
ORBITAL PERIOD: 384.8 days
DETECTION METHOD: Transit

O

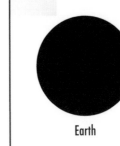

Earth

Scientists
think this
planet
might be
covered in a
giant ocean.

KEPLER-22 B

MASS: 36 Earths
ORBITAL RADIUS: 0.849 AU
ECCENTRICITY: 0.0
DISCOVERY DATE: 2011

PLANET RADIUS: 0.212 x Jupiter
ORBITAL PERIOD: 289.9 days
DETECTION METHOD: Transit

P

Earth

KOI-3503 B

MASS: 9.2 Earths
ORBITAL RADIUS: 0.1462 AU
ECCENTRICITY: 0.0
DISCOVERY DATE: 2021

PLANET RADIUS: 1.19 x Earth
ORBITAL PERIOD: 21.2 days
DETECTION METHOD: Transit

Earth

EPLER-1142 B

MASS: 2.76 Earths
ORBITAL RADIUS: 0.1343 AU
ECCENTRICITY: 0.0
DISCOVERY DATE: 2016

PLANET RADIUS: 1.47 x Earth
ORBITAL PERIOD: 18.3 days
DETECTION METHOD: Transit

U

Earth

KEPLER-1079 B

MASS: 3.29 Earths
ORBITAL RADIUS: 0.1092 AU
ECCENTRICITY: 0.0
DISCOVERY DATE: 2016

PLANET RADIUS: 1.63 x Earth
ORBITAL PERIOD: 13.2 days
DETECTION METHOD: Transit

V

Earth

EPIC 201841433 B

MASS: 1.12 Earths
ORBITAL RADIUS: 0.035 AU
ECCENTRICITY: 0.0
DISCOVERY DATE: 2019

PLANET RADIUS: 1.04 x Earth
ORBITAL PERIOD: 4.2 days
DETECTION METHOD: Transit

TYPE 4:

Terrestrial

In our solar system, Mercury, Venus, Earth, and Mars are terrestrial planets. Terrestrial planets are also called rocky planets. For the planets outside our solar system—exoplanets—terrestrial planets are Earth-sized and smaller.

Terrestrial planets must have a hard surface. These planets are made of silicate, rock, water, and/or carbon. Terrestrial exoplanets twice the size of Earth or larger are called super-Earths (see page 30).

ANY LIKE EARTH?

So far, scientists haven't discovered a planet quite like Earth, but our knowledge is expanding constantly. Exoplanet systems like TRAPPIST-1, which contains seven rocky terrestrial worlds—the most Earth-sized planets found in the habitable zone of a single star—was an amazing discovery from just 2017. Such discoveries will expand our understanding not only of exoplanets but of the universe in which we live.

GOOD COMPANY

Scientists believe there could be more than 10,000,000,000 terrestrial planets in our galaxy alone.

CORE

SILICATE MANTLE

HARD SURFACE

HABITABILITY

Terrestrial exoplanets may have gaseous atmospheres, but that is not a defining feature. More investigation is needed to discover if these rocky planets have atmospheres, oceans, mild temperatures, and other signs of habitability.

MEET SOME TERRESTRIAL EXOPLANETS

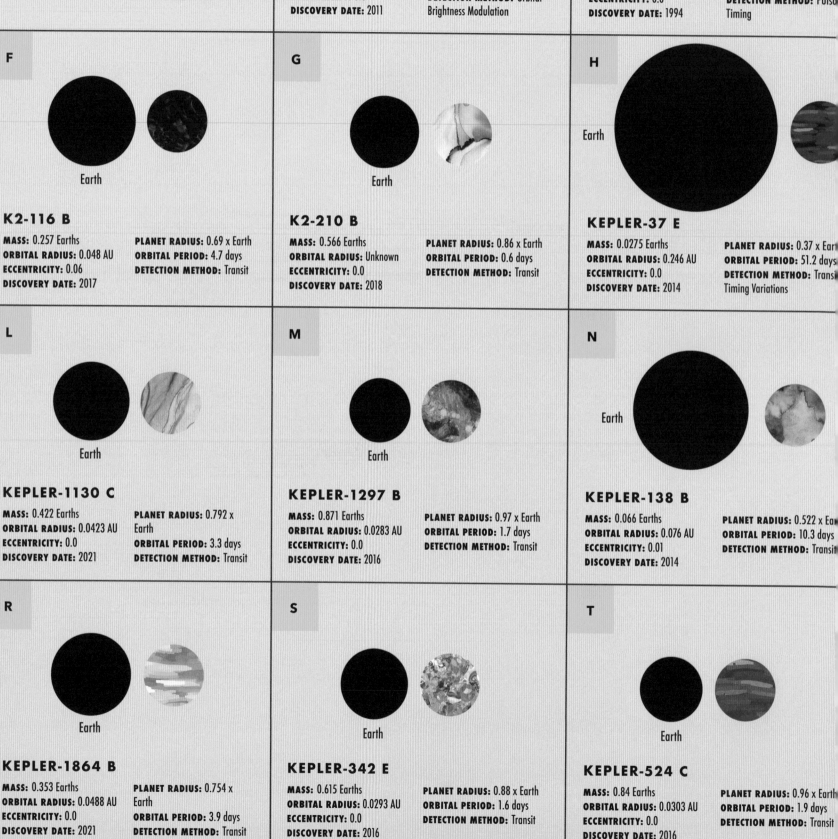

A

Earth

One of the hottest planets yet to be discovered, KOI-55 b is hotter than even the sun! In fact, the entire planet is slowly evaporating.

KOI-55 B

MASS: 0.44 Earths
ORBITAL RADIUS: 0.006 AU
ECCENTRICITY: 0.0
DISCOVERY DATE: 2011

PLANET RADIUS: 0.759 x Earth
ORBITAL PERIOD: 0.2 days
DETECTION METHOD: Orbital Brightness Modulation

B

Earth

Though one of the first exoplanets to be discovered, PSR B1257+12 b is among the most inhospitable; it's bombarded by deadly radiation.

PSR B1257+12 B

MASS: 0.02 Earths
ORBITAL RADIUS: 0.19 AU
ECCENTRICITY: 0.0
DISCOVERY DATE: 1994

PLANET RADIUS: 0.338 x Ea
ORBITAL PERIOD: 25.3 day
DETECTION METHOD: Pulsa Timing

F

Earth

K2-116 B

MASS: 0.257 Earths
ORBITAL RADIUS: 0.048 AU
ECCENTRICITY: 0.06
DISCOVERY DATE: 2017

PLANET RADIUS: 0.69 x Earth
ORBITAL PERIOD: 4.7 days
DETECTION METHOD: Transit

G

Earth

K2-210 B

MASS: 0.566 Earths
ORBITAL RADIUS: Unknown
ECCENTRICITY: 0.0
DISCOVERY DATE: 2018

PLANET RADIUS: 0.86 x Earth
ORBITAL PERIOD: 0.6 days
DETECTION METHOD: Transit

H

Earth

KEPLER-37 E

MASS: 0.0275 Earths
ORBITAL RADIUS: 0.246 AU
ECCENTRICITY: 0.0
DISCOVERY DATE: 2014

PLANET RADIUS: 0.37 x Eart
ORBITAL PERIOD: 51.2 days
DETECTION METHOD: Transi Timing Variations

L

Earth

KEPLER-1130 C

MASS: 0.422 Earths
ORBITAL RADIUS: 0.0423 AU
ECCENTRICITY: 0.0
DISCOVERY DATE: 2021

PLANET RADIUS: 0.792 x Earth
ORBITAL PERIOD: 3.3 days
DETECTION METHOD: Transit

M

Earth

KEPLER-1297 B

MASS: 0.871 Earths
ORBITAL RADIUS: 0.0283 AU
ECCENTRICITY: 0.0
DISCOVERY DATE: 2016

PLANET RADIUS: 0.97 x Earth
ORBITAL PERIOD: 1.7 days
DETECTION METHOD: Transit

N

Earth

KEPLER-138 B

MASS: 0.066 Earths
ORBITAL RADIUS: 0.076 AU
ECCENTRICITY: 0.01
DISCOVERY DATE: 2014

PLANET RADIUS: 0.522 x Ear
ORBITAL PERIOD: 10.3 days
DETECTION METHOD: Transit

R

Earth

KEPLER-1864 B

MASS: 0.353 Earths
ORBITAL RADIUS: 0.0488 AU
ECCENTRICITY: 0.0
DISCOVERY DATE: 2021

PLANET RADIUS: 0.754 x Earth
ORBITAL PERIOD: 3.9 days
DETECTION METHOD: Transit

S

Earth

KEPLER-342 E

MASS: 0.615 Earths
ORBITAL RADIUS: 0.0293 AU
ECCENTRICITY: 0.0
DISCOVERY DATE: 2016

PLANET RADIUS: 0.88 x Earth
ORBITAL PERIOD: 1.6 days
DETECTION METHOD: Transit

T

Earth

KEPLER-524 C

MASS: 0.84 Earths
ORBITAL RADIUS: 0.0303 AU
ECCENTRICITY: 0.0
DISCOVERY DATE: 2016

PLANET RADIUS: 0.96 x Earth
ORBITAL PERIOD: 1.9 days
DETECTION METHOD: Transit

DISTANCE FROM EARTH IN LIGHT-YEARS

Earth

W U V N
D F E H

G

L
C I R

J

B Q

K P

0   500   1,000   1,500   2,000

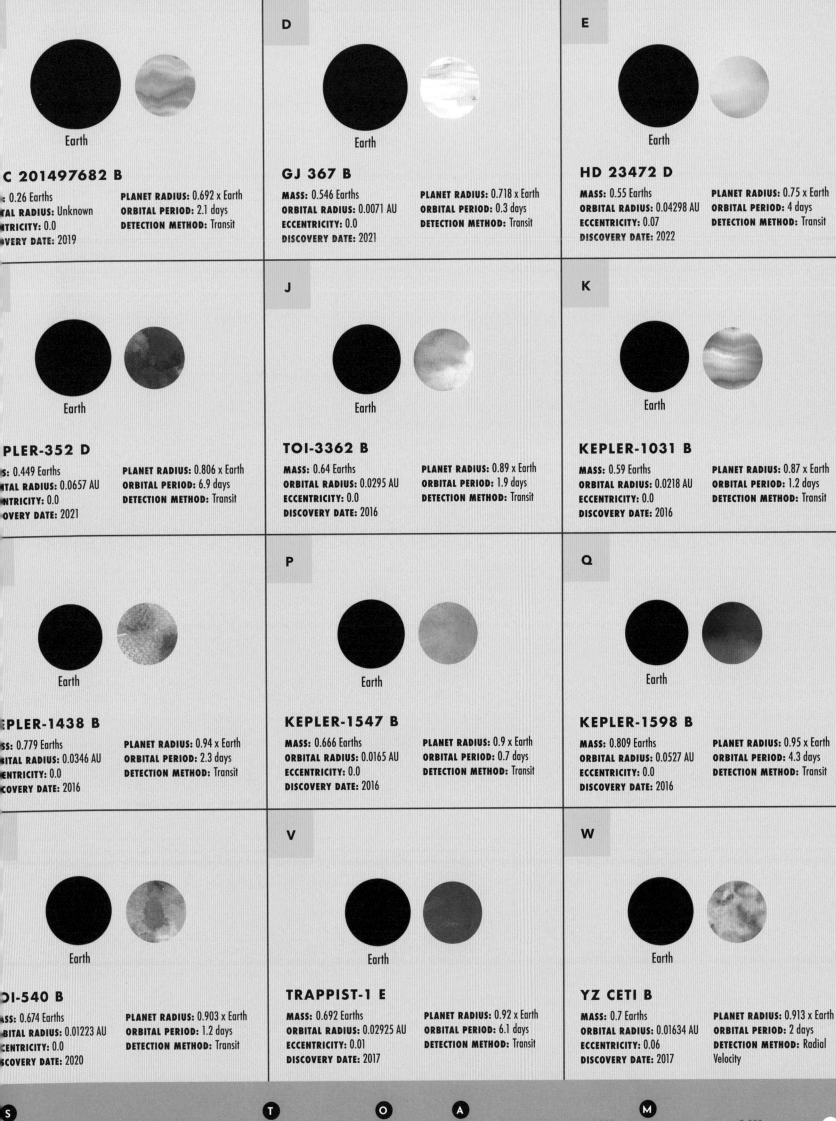

C 201497682 B

Earth

: 0.26 Earths
TAL RADIUS: Unknown
TRICITY: 0.0
VERY DATE: 2019

PLANET RADIUS: 0.692 x Earth
ORBITAL PERIOD: 2.1 days
DETECTION METHOD: Transit

D

Earth

GJ 367 B

MASS: 0.546 Earths
ORBITAL RADIUS: 0.0071 AU
ECCENTRICITY: 0.0
DISCOVERY DATE: 2021

PLANET RADIUS: 0.718 x Earth
ORBITAL PERIOD: 0.3 days
DETECTION METHOD: Transit

E

Earth

HD 23472 D

MASS: 0.55 Earths
ORBITAL RADIUS: 0.04298 AU
ECCENTRICITY: 0.07
DISCOVERY DATE: 2022

PLANET RADIUS: 0.75 x Earth
ORBITAL PERIOD: 4 days
DETECTION METHOD: Transit

Earth

PLER-352 D

: 0.449 Earths
TAL RADIUS: 0.0657 AU
TRICITY: 0.0
OVERY DATE: 2021

PLANET RADIUS: 0.806 x Earth
ORBITAL PERIOD: 6.9 days
DETECTION METHOD: Transit

J

Earth

TOI-3362 B

MASS: 0.64 Earths
ORBITAL RADIUS: 0.0295 AU
ECCENTRICITY: 0.0
DISCOVERY DATE: 2016

PLANET RADIUS: 0.89 x Earth
ORBITAL PERIOD: 1.9 days
DETECTION METHOD: Transit

K

Earth

KEPLER-1031 B

MASS: 0.59 Earths
ORBITAL RADIUS: 0.0218 AU
ECCENTRICITY: 0.0
DISCOVERY DATE: 2016

PLANET RADIUS: 0.87 x Earth
ORBITAL PERIOD: 1.2 days
DETECTION METHOD: Transit

Earth

EPLER-1438 B

SS: 0.779 Earths
RITAL RADIUS: 0.0346 AU
ENTRICITY: 0.0
COVERY DATE: 2016

PLANET RADIUS: 0.94 x Earth
ORBITAL PERIOD: 2.3 days
DETECTION METHOD: Transit

P

Earth

KEPLER-1547 B

MASS: 0.666 Earths
ORBITAL RADIUS: 0.0165 AU
ECCENTRICITY: 0.0
DISCOVERY DATE: 2016

PLANET RADIUS: 0.9 x Earth
ORBITAL PERIOD: 0.7 days
DETECTION METHOD: Transit

Q

Earth

KEPLER-1598 B

MASS: 0.809 Earths
ORBITAL RADIUS: 0.0527 AU
ECCENTRICITY: 0.0
DISCOVERY DATE: 2016

PLANET RADIUS: 0.95 x Earth
ORBITAL PERIOD: 4.3 days
DETECTION METHOD: Transit

Earth

OI-540 B

ASS: 0.674 Earths
BITAL RADIUS: 0.01223 AU
CENTRICITY: 0.0
SCOVERY DATE: 2020

PLANET RADIUS: 0.903 x Earth
ORBITAL PERIOD: 1.2 days
DETECTION METHOD: Transit

V

Earth

TRAPPIST-1 E

MASS: 0.692 Earths
ORBITAL RADIUS: 0.02925 AU
ECCENTRICITY: 0.01
DISCOVERY DATE: 2017

PLANET RADIUS: 0.92 x Earth
ORBITAL PERIOD: 6.1 days
DETECTION METHOD: Transit

W

Earth

YZ CETI B

MASS: 0.7 Earths
ORBITAL RADIUS: 0.01634 AU
ECCENTRICITY: 0.06
DISCOVERY DATE: 2017

PLANET RADIUS: 0.913 x Earth
ORBITAL PERIOD: 2 days
DETECTION METHOD: Radial Velocity

Glossary

astrometry: a method for finding exoplanets that looks for tiny changes in a star's location caused by an exoplanet's gravity

coronography: a method used to block a star's light in order to take more accurate pictures of its planets

direct imaging: using high-power telescopes to take pictures of exoplanets

Doppler effect: when sound or light waves squeeze or stretch because of the movement of the object making them

exoplanet: a planet located outside our solar system

galaxy: a collection of solar systems

gas giant: the largest type of exoplanet, composed mainly of gas

gravitational microlensing: a method for detecting exoplanets that looks for changes in a star's brightness caused by double images

habitable: capable of supporting life as we know it

habitable zone: the orbital band around a star where temperatures would allow liquid water and life to exist

hot Jupiter: a gas giant exoplanet located very close to its star

James Webb Space Telescope: a new telescope launched by NASA in 2022 with special capabilities for detecting and learning about exoplanets

light-year: the distance that light can travel in the space of one year (around 6,000,000,000,000 miles)

mini-Neptune: an exoplanet that is smaller than Neptune but larger than Earth

Neptunian: the second-largest type of exoplanet, composed mainly of gas

Neptunian Desert: the extremely hot area close to a star where no Neptune-sized planets are expected to survive

orbit: the path a planet takes around its star

probability: a branch of mathematics that explains how likely something is to happen

radial velocity: a method for detecting exoplanets by looking for stars impacted by a planet's gravity

rogue planet: a planet that drifts and doesn't have a regular orbit around a star

solar system: a star and all of its orbiting planets, moons, asteroids, comet material, rocks, and dust

spectroscopy: a method of determining the composition of an exoplanet by reading the color and pattern of light waves that pass through the planet's atmosphere

starshade: a theoretical device that could be used to block a star's light from interfering with a space-based telescope

super-Earth: the third-largest type of exoplanet, larger than Earth and often rocky

terrestrial: the smallest type of exoplanet, always rocky and Earth-sized or smaller

transit method: a way to detect exoplanets by looking for variations in the brightness of a star

universe: the entire existence of space, made of all the galaxies put together

ABOUT THE AUTHOR

Wendy Bjazevich is the author of the Green and Small series and is a science enthusiast. She received a B.S. from Brigham Young University in sociology and health education and a Master of Forensic Sciences from George Washington University. Wendy enjoys spending time with her husband and six children.

ABOUT THE ILLUSTRATOR

David Miles is an award-winning and bestselling author and illustrator of over 40 books, including *The Side-by-Side Declaration of Independence*, *Book*, *The Interactive Constitution*, *Allegro*, *Unicorn and Horse*, and other titles. He has worked as a designer, illustrator, and creative director, and he now runs Bushel & Peck Books with his wife, Stephanie. He's been named a CYBILS Award Finalist, Publishers Weekly Star Watch Nominee, Trvst Changemaker, New York Book Show Award Winner, and Bill Fisher Award Finalist, among other accolades. He lives in Fresno, California, with his family.

SOURCES CONSULTED

Anne Marie Helmenstine, Ph.D. "Spectroscopy Definition." ThoughtCo, September 13, 2019. https://www.thoughtco.com/definition-of-spectroscopy-605676.

Bock, Michael. "Curious Universe: Let's Go Planet-Hunting!" NASA. NASA, July 12, 2021. https://www.nasa.gov/mediacast/let-s-go-planet-hunting.

Cimone, Matthew. "The Color of Habitable Worlds." Universe Today, October 30, 2020. https://www.universetoday.com/148532/the-color-of-habitable-worlds/.

"The Different Kinds of Exoplanets You Meet in the Milky Way." The Planetary Society, n.d. https://www.planetary.org/articles/the-different-kinds-of-exoplanets-you-meet-in-the-milky-way.

E, Phillip. "What Is the Order from Largest to Smallest: Galaxy, Universe, Star, Asteroids, Planets, Moons, Solar System?: Socratic." Socratic.org, May 19, 2017. https://socratic.org/questions/what-is-the-order-from-largest-to-smallest-galaxy-universe-star-asteroids-planet.

"Exoplanet Exploration: Planets beyond Our Solar System." NASA, December 17, 2015. https://exoplanets.nasa.gov/.

"Exoplanet Facts for Kids - Interesting Facts about Exoplanets." Planets for Kids, June 17, 2019. https://www.planetsforkids.org/the-universe/exoplanets.html.

"Exoplanets Planets Facts for Kids: Summary, Structure & Formation." The Nine Planets, November 19, 2020. https://nineplanets.org/kids/exoplanets-planets/.

"Exoplanets." ESA, n.d. https://www.esa.int/kids/en/learn/Life_in_Space/Are_we_alone/Exoplanets.

"'Forbidden Planet' Discovery Amazes Scientists." KidsNews, May 30, 2019. https://www.kidsnews.com.au/space/newly-found-extreme-world-nicknamed-the-forbidden-planet-would-melt-a-human-in-under-a-second/news-story/9bd5a46aec9ff8cbf242c4a0a dc02928.

"Gas Giant." Gas giant - Academic Kids, n.d. https://academickids.com/encyclopedia/index.php/Gas_giant.

"Nancy Grace Roman Space Telescope." NASA, n.d. https://roman.gsfc.nasa.gov/exoplanets_direct_imaging.html.

"Navigation." ESA Science & Technology - Exoplanet detection methods, n.d. https://sci.esa.int/web/exoplanets/-/60655-detection-methods.

"Planets." NASA, July 14, 2021. https://solarsystem.nasa.gov/planets/overview/.

"Probability." Wikipedia. Wikimedia Foundation, November 23, 2022. https://en.wikipedia.org/wiki/Probability.

"Probably Probability." Mensa for Kids, n.d. https://www.mensaforkids.org/teach/lesson-plans/probably-probability/.

"Solar System, Galaxy, Universe: What's the Difference?" NASA, n.d. https://nightsky.jpl.nasa.gov/news-display.cfm?News_ID=573.

Starr, Michelle. "In a First, Astronomers Find an Exoplanet by Using Radio Waves and a Wobbly Star." ScienceAlert, August 5, 2020. https://www.sciencealert.com/for-the-first-time-a-radio-telescope-has-been-used-to-find-a-planet-by-its-wiggling-star.

"Terrestrial Planet Facts for Kids - the Inner Planets." Planets for Kids, July 10, 2019. https://www.planetsforkids.org/planet/terrestrial-planets.html.

Wall, Mike. "Astronomers Find Record-Breaking Haul of Starless 'Rogue' Planets." Space.com. Space, December 22, 2021. https://www.space.com/rogue-exoplanets-record-breaking-haul.

"What Is a 'Super Earth' and Why Do We Care?" Discovery, n.d. https://www.discovery.com/space/what-is-a--super-earth---and-why-do-we-care-.

"What Is an Exoplanet?" Wonderopolis, n.d. https://wonderopolis.org/wonder/what-is-an-exoplanet.

BUSHEL
& PECK
BOOKS

ABOUT BUSHEL & PECK BOOKS

Bushel & Peck Books is a children's publishing house with a special mission. Through our Book-for-Book Promise™, we donate one book to kids in need for every book we sell. Our beautiful books are given to kids through schools, libraries, local neighborhoods, shelters, nonprofits, and also to many selfless organizations who are working hard to make a difference. So thank you for purchasing this book! Because of you, another book will find its way into the hands of a child who needs it most.

WHY LITERACY MATTERS

We can't solve every problem in the world, but we believe children's books can help. Illiteracy is linked to many of the world's greatest challenges, including crime, school dropout rates, and drug use. Yet impressively, just the presence of books in a home can be a leg up for struggling kids. According to one study, "Children growing up in homes with many books get three years more schooling than children from bookless homes, independent of their parents' education, occupation, and class. This is as great an advantage as having university educated rather than unschooled parents, and twice the advantage of having a professional rather than an unskilled father."[1]

Unfortunately, many children in need find themselves without adequate access to age-appropriate books. One study found that low-income neighborhoods have, in some US cities, only one book for every three hundred kids (compared to thirteen books for every one child in middle-income neighborhoods).[2]

With our Book-for-Book Promise™, Bushel & Peck Books is putting quality children's books into the hands of as many kids as possible. We hope these books bring an increased interest in reading and learning, and with that, a greater chance for future success.

NOMINATE A SCHOOL OR ORGANIZATION
TO RECEIVE FREE BOOKS

Do you know a school, library, or organization that could use some free books for their kids? We'd love to help! Please fill out the nomination form at www.bushelandpeckbooks.com, and we'll do everything we can to make something happen.

---

1   M.D.R. Evans, Jonathan Kelley, Joanna Sikora & Donald J. Treiman. Family scholarly culture and educational success: Books and schooling in 27 nations. *Research in Social Stratification and Mobility.* Volume 28, Issue 2, 2010. 171–197.

2   Neuman, S.B. & D. Celano (2006). The knowledge gap: Effects of leveling the playing field for low- and middle-income children. *Reading Research Quarterly,* 176–201.